THORNTON WILDER

LUCRECE

FROM 'LE VIOL DE LUCRÈCE' BY
ANDRÉ OBEY

BOSTON AND NEW YORK

HOUGHTON MIFFLIN COMPANY

The Riverside Press Cambridge

1933

The Riverside Press
CAMBRIDGE · MASSACHUSETTS
PRINTED IN THE U.S.A.

'Lucrece' received its first performance at the Hanna Theatre, Cleveland, Ohio, November 29, 1932.

It opened in New York City at the Belasco Theatre, Tuesday evening, December 20, 1932. It was presented by Katharine Cornell; directed by Guthrie McClintic; with settings and costumes by Robert Edmond Jones; and with music by Deems Taylor. The cast was as follows:

First Soldier	WILLIAM J. TANNEN
Second Soldier	GEORGE MACREADY
Tarquin	BRIAN AHERNE
Collatine	PEDRO DE CORDOBA
Brutus	CHARLES WALDRON
First Narrator	BLANCHE YURKA
Lucrece	KATHARINE CORNELL
Julia	KATHLEEN CHASE
Emilia	JOYCE CAREY
Sidonia	HARRIET INGERSOLL
Marina	BRENDA FORBES
Second Narrator	ROBERT LORAINE
Valerius	GEORGE MACREADY
First Servant	FRANCIS MORAN
Second Servant	BARRY MAHOOL
Third Servant	CHARLES THORNE

Miss Cornell and Mr. McClintic acknowledged Miss Martha Graham's valuable assistance in the production.

'Le Viol de Lucrèce' was first presented by the Compagnie des Quinze at the Théâtre du Vieux-Colombier in Paris on the twelfth of March, 1931.

LUCRECE
ACT ONE

CHARACTERS

LUCRECE

EMILIA

SIDONIA

JULIA

MARINA

TARQUIN

COLLATINE

BRUTUS

VALERIUS

TWO NARRATORS

SOLDIERS, SERVANTS, ETC.

☙ SCENES ☙

✠ LUCRECE ✠

ACT ONE
SCENE ONE

Before the curtain.

TWO SOLDIERS *are on guard. One at the right, the other at the left.*

At the right from between the edge of the curtain and the proscenium pillar, a bright light falls upon the stage. This opening represents the door of a Roman tent.

Laughter, cheers and applause issue from within.

FIRST SOLDIER (*at the left*). Hsst — Hey!

SECOND SOLDIER (*at the right*). Well, what is it?

FIRST SOLDIER. What's going on in there?

SECOND SOLDIER. The Lieutenant Collatine is giving a dinner for his friends.

FIRST SOLDIER. I know! Some people manage to have a good time when there's a war going on!

3

SECOND SOLDIER. Well, why don't you hurry and rise in the ranks yourself?

Cheers from the tent.

FIRST SOLDIER. What's the cheering for?

SECOND SOLDIER. Enjoying themselves. Pleased about something.

FIRST SOLDIER. ... about what?

SECOND SOLDIER. They forgot to tell me.

FIRST SOLDIER. What are they doing?

SECOND SOLDIER. Drinking.

FIRST SOLDIER. Their luck.

Burst of joyous din from the tent.

How many are there?

SECOND SOLDIER. Wait a minute! (*He takes a step forward and cautiously extends his head toward the light.*) There's Collatine, naturally... and Sicinius... (*laughing*)... and there's Brutus — Junius Brutus.

FIRST SOLDIER (*laughing too*). What, is Brutus there?... Oh, he's a character. There's no one like him!

SECOND SOLDIER. Then there's another, but I can't see his face... I see my Lord Tarquin.

FIRST SOLDIER. Ai! Look out for yourself! I wouldn't like to get caught crossing his path — especially when he's out on one of his little private expeditions.

SECOND SOLDIER. That makes five in all.

FIRST SOLDIER. Only five? Only five make all that noise? You'd think there were forty.

SECOND SOLDIER. Even then, there's one there that scarcely makes a sound...

FIRST SOLDIER. Tarquin. Tarquin, eh?

SECOND SOLDIER. How'd you know?

FIRST SOLDIER. That's a thing you'd know right off. He never enjoys himself like other people. Did you ever see Tarquin laugh? Really laugh out loud?

SECOND SOLDIER. Look out! — Brutus is getting up. He's going to make a speech. Keep quiet now and I'll tell you what he says.

> *Silence.*
>
> *Then from the tent issues the sound of a voice engaged in formal oratory.*
>
> *The* SECOND SOLDIER *doubles up with mirth.*

FIRST SOLDIER. What's he saying?

SECOND SOLDIER. Oh! Oh! Oh! — That Brutus! What a speaker!

More oratory.

... Never! Couldn't have!...

FIRST SOLDIER. What does he say? Tell me!

SECOND SOLDIER. Be quiet. I can't hear anything.

The voice seems to draw to a close. Applause.

Oh! Oh! (*He takes advantage of the noise to report what he has heard.*) Listen, last night they all went to Rome. Every one of them, and some more besides. Secretly, see, without telling a soul. A sort of surprise raid on their homes. It was this way: they'd made a kind of... a kind of what-they-call a wager. A wager on which of their wives behaved best while they were away. They went back to see what was going on in their homes. Oh!! Brutus was telling about it. Seems like they saw some things they didn't look for...

FIRST SOLDIER. What, what?

SECOND SOLDIER. Sh! Brutus has begun again.

The voice within the tent resumes its oratory.

The SECOND SOLDIER *now reports the speech, phrase by phrase.*

'Cornelia they found giving a supper...'

FIRST SOLDIER. Ha! Ha!

SECOND SOLDIER. 'Ligeia had gone to a ball...'

FIRST SOLDIER. Ho! Ho!

SECOND SOLDIER. 'Calpurnia...' Oh — 'they found lying crossways on her bed stark naked...'

FIRST SOLDIER. Hu! Hu!

SECOND SOLDIER. ... 'drunk as a lord. And Portia' — wait a minute...

FIRST SOLDIER. What, what?

SECOND SOLDIER. They spent a whole hour looking for her, high and low. And they couldn't find her anywhere.

FIRST SOLDIER (*at a high pitch of enthusiasm*). Ho! Ho! — What else! What else!

> BRUTUS *continues speaking within.*

Tell me.

SECOND SOLDIER. Don't talk, I tell you!

FIRST SOLDIER. What's he saying?

SECOND SOLDIER (*angry*). How can I hear anything while you keep on talking! Be quiet, can't you?

> BRUTUS'S *discourse has now changed to the slow and measured.*

> *The* SECOND SOLDIER *begins to sigh in admiration and sympathy.*

That's something! — Think of that! Collatine must

7

have been proud. (*To his companion.*) Listen, Collatine's wife...

FIRST SOLDIER. Lucrece?

SECOND SOLDIER. Yes, Lucrece. They found her sitting among the women of the house — all of them spinning away — That's something like!

FIRST SOLDIER. Does that mean that Collatine won the wager?

SECOND SOLDIER. Wait! (*He listens again.*) Brutus says he never saw a more beautiful sight, he says: More peaceful, he says — (*Changing his tone abruptly.*) But why should Tarquin look like that! You should see the look on Tarquin's face!

FIRST SOLDIER. He's jealous.

SECOND SOLDIER. Jealous? What of?

FIRST SOLDIER. Of Collatine. 'What!' he's saying to himself. 'A mere under-officer have a beautiful wife like that,' he says, 'while I, the King's son, still haven't found any!' That's what he's saying.

SECOND SOLDIER (*incredulous*). How do *you* know?

FIRST SOLDIER. Don't talk to me! I know him. Last year I had to be in his body-guard...

LUCRECE

SECOND SOLDIER (*listening again*). Sh! Let me listen! — Ah, Brutus can talk!... He's describing just what it looked like: Lucrece in her house. The women spinning. The quiet and everything. Oh, that fellow's an orator. If he only wanted to, he could... (*Listens.*) Oh... oh... He says: It was a spectacle that he can only call Roman. Conveying... no, I mean displaying... at the same time Grandeur and Simplicity. (*With enthusiasm.*) Oh, listen to that! 'A man can carry all his courage to the camp, when he knows he leaves at home the virtue of a Lucrece.' (*Excitedly.*) Hey! Hey!

FIRST SOLDIER. Bravo!

> *Applause from the tent.*

They're all applauding him now. Hear them?

BOTH SOLDIERS} To Lucrece! Long live the chaste Lucrece!

SECOND SOLDIER. Hst! Look out! Here comes Tarquin!

> *He quickly moves away from the opening of the tent. The two* SOLDIERS *stand motionless in their places.*
>
> TARQUIN *emerges from the tent, and walks slowly toward the centre of the stage: then begins to stride sombrely to and fro the length of the proscenium.*
>
> *A slight pause. Sound of voices approaching from the tent.*
>
> TARQUIN *leaves the stage, at the left. A number of* OFFICERS *enter gaily, taking leave of* COLLATINE *at the door of his tent.*

9

OFFICERS. Good night — Good night, happy husband. Good night. The most fortunate husband in Rome.

COLLATINE. Good night, good night, my friends. And to you, many thanks, my dear Brutus.

BRUTUS. You think of me as always joking.

> COLLATINE *and the* OFFICERS *burst out laughing.*

... It's true: I like to joke and laugh, yes, and at times to make fun of lots of things in life. But at least there's one thing that I always take seriously — yes, even solemnly — Rome!! Rome, my friends, and its strength and glory. My dear friend Collatine: Lucrece, your Lucrece is the fairest ornament of all Rome.

ALL. It's true. It's the truth!

BRUTUS (*embracing* COLLATINE). There, good night!

ALL. Good night! Good night!

COLLATINE. Good night, Brutus.

> *The* OFFICERS *cross the stage and go out, talking.*

> COLLATINE *follows them a few steps, then returns to his tent, singing under his breath, and disappears.*

> *A pause.*

> TARQUIN *emerges from the shadow: he softly approaches the tent. A trumpet call is heard in the distance. The light in Collatine's tent is extinguished. The stage is lighted only by the red gleam of some campfire. Another trumpet call.*

TARQUIN (*to the* FIRST SOLDIER). You, there!

FIRST SOLDIER (*moving toward him*). My lord?

TARQUIN. My horse.

> *The* SOLDIERS *go out.*
>
> TARQUIN *slowly follows them.*
>
> **THE CURTAIN RISES**

SCENE TWO

A room in the house of COLLATINE.

*At the back, seated among her women on a
platform,* LUCRECE *is spinning. Her maids
are* JULIA, EMILIA, SIDONIA, *and* MARINA.
EMILIA *is the chief among them.*

At the right at the front of the stage, the
FIRST NARRATOR, *a woman wearing a
mask, is sitting on the ground against the wall,
her head turned toward* LUCRECE.

FIRST NARRATOR. Lucrece is spinning. Surrounded by the
women of her household, she is spinning. As she does
every evening; as she did last night, and the night before.
... She ate her dinner alone... smiling. Alone, silent and
smiling.... She is the least bit greedy and the trout that
had been touched with herbs was even more delicious
than usual. After dinner she went into the kitchen to
pay her compliment to the cook. She found the great
white kitchen washed and scrubbed and ready for tomorrow. You may be sure there wasn't the slightest
odour of fish. Lucrece has a sensitive nose. Then she
went over the household books with the steward. And
now she has called her maids together and she is spinning.
It is ten o'clock. In the best ordered house in Rome, all
is well.

JULIA. Emilia is tangling the thread.

EMILIA. And Sidonia is breaking it, which is worse.

SIDONIA. Marina! — Marina is thinking about her lover.

MARINA. And Julia is yawning. Oh, how she is yawning!

EMILIA ⎫
SIDONIA ⎬ Look, my lady, look how she is yawning.
MARINA ⎭

> *Enter the* SECOND NARRATOR, *a man wearing a mask. He enters from the left.*

SECOND NARRATOR. Tarquin has called for his horse and has left the camp. My Lord Tarquin, the King's son, the future King of Rome, has left the camp and the army behind him.... It is true that last night he persuaded his officers to come on some ridiculous excursion. But to-night he has set off alone, and I am afraid (yes, I am afraid) that there is some disastrous plan behind it all.... Why should he gallop so! Can you not hear him? Can not you hear the iron hoofs of his horse ringing on the long Roman road?... Where is he going? Where can he be going? Why is he spurring his horse so? Why must he kill his horse under him with such urging?

SIDONIA. Twenty-seven ... twenty-eight ... twenty-nine ... thirty.

EMILIA. Sh!

SIDONIA. ... Thirty-one ... thirty-two ...

EMILIA
MARINA } Don't count out loud, Sidonia.
JULIA

SIDONIA. I'm counting my strands.

EMILIA. Then count them to yourself.

SECOND NARRATOR. What, what was that? His horse stumbled. Nothing serious. Only that log in the way.... Come, now, Tarquin, let him walk. Listen to him, feel how he is panting between your knees.... Come, it's time to go back, Tarquin. Surely that's enough. This late ride has been good exercise. A long siege like this one before Ardea is apt to make a soldier's blood run sluggish. I can understand how a king's son, a great cavalry leader, I can imagine how he must steal off for an occasional hour of galloping. He can think himself in full charge at the head of his squadron. But now, surely it's time to go back. Let us turn our horse's head. We are streaming with sweat. Our groom will rub us down with a coarse glove. We will sleep like a log until the roll of drums at five in the morning. What, Tarquin? It's time to go back.

EMILIA. Sidonia's thoughts are miles away. She is dreaming.

EMILIA
JULIA } Sidonia!
MARINA

MARINA. What are you thinking about?

14

SIDONIA. I was thinking of last night, and all those officers in their golden armour...

EMILIA
JULIA   } ...All those officers in their golden armour...
MARINA

LUCRECE (*smiling*). Sh — sh — sh!

FIRST NARRATOR. Come, come, my children. Back to our work... Spin, as we were spinning last night and the night before, and as we shall be spinning tomorrow night and the night after.

SECOND NARRATOR. He's started galloping again! And it's Rome he's bound for! He gives a yell and lashes his exhausted horse.... Rome? For Rome?... What is it — desertion? is there a conspiracy afoot? Treachery? Is there some meeting, or is it to surprise someone? Yes, he was at Rome last night. But tonight he's alone! And why, tonight?

SIDONIA. Fifteen... sixteen... seventeen... eighteen!

EMILIA. Again!

SIDONIA. Nineteen... twenty! I'm counting my strands, I tell you.

EMILIA. And I tell you to do it to yourself.

SIDONIA. Sh— twenty-one! When I do it to myself I can't keep track — twenty-two! Twenty-three!

EMILIA. No, please be quiet.

SIDONIA (*louder*). Twenty-four! Twenty-five!

EMILIA (*appealing to* LUCRECE). My lady!

LUCRECE. Ha! Ha! Ha! Ha!

SIDONIA. Twenty-six! Twenty-seven! Twenty-eight!

MARINA
JULIA } (*gaily*). That's enough.

SIDONIA. Twenty-nine!

MARINA
JULIA } Enough! Enough!
EMILIA

SECOND NARRATOR. Tarquin is entering Rome by the Nomentian Gate.

SIDONIA (*crying out*). Thirty. Help me, my lady. They're trying to upset me in my count.

SECOND NARRATOR. I can hear the horse's hoofs in the deserted streets...

SIDONIA. Thirty! Thirty! Thirty!

MARINA. No, thirty-two!

JULIA. Thirty-six.

LUCRECE

EMILIA. Thirty-nine!

SECOND NARRATOR. ... crossing the sleeping squares. The beat of the hoofs rings every moment more clearly and more coldly.

SIDONIA. My lady, please help me hold on to my thirty.

SECOND NARRATOR. On guard everyone! He is here!

> *Knocking at a door.* LUCRECE *and her servants turn toward the left.*

FIRST NARRATOR. What! A visitor! At this hour?

> *A* SERVANT *enters from the left. He is carrying a torch.*

SERVANT. My Lord Tarquin.

> *Enter* TARQUIN.

> *The* WOMEN *rise and make a deep curtsey. They then descend from the platform where* LUCRECE *remains seated alone.*

FIRST NARRATOR. Is there bad news?... Has there been an accident... some quarrel... Is her husband wounded? What? What is it? What is it?

> TARQUIN *approaches* LUCRECE *slowly. She rises.*

Collatine? Collatine? Our beloved Collatine, what of him? Speak, Tarquin!

> LUCRECE *descends from the platform and joins* TARQUIN.

17

SECOND NARRATOR. Collatine is wonderfully well, as always.

> TARQUIN *bows before* LUCRECE.

We must talk about Collatine, it seems! Yes, listen to him... treacherous and hypocritical... 'Collatine fights like a lion. Collatine is strong as a Turk! Collatine is handsome as a god!'... to think that a king's son could...

> LUCRECE, *followed by the* FIRST NARRATOR, *and* TARQUIN, *followed by the* SECOND NARRATOR, *have moved forward toward the audience.*

> FIRST NARRATOR, *as* LUCRECE *smiles at* TARQUIN, *who bows his head:*

FIRST NARRATOR. For a king's son one must prepare one's best and most respectful welcome! This house is his own. (*She — the* FIRST NARRATOR *— moves to the left of the stage.*) So!

SECOND NARRATOR (*moving to the right*). Alas!
> LUCRECE *and* TARQUIN *turn their backs upon the audience and slowly return to the platform.*

SECOND NARRATOR. Alas! He is saying that urgent business has recalled him to Rome.

FIRST NARRATOR. She is remembering all that Roman hospitality comprises of courtesy and thoughtfulness.

SECOND NARRATOR. He is saying that he is burdened with the cares of royalty.

FIRST NARRATOR. She is wondering if the steward is aware of all that must be done for a royal guest.

SECOND NARRATOR. He says that he is tired and will be glad to sleep tonight.

FIRST NARRATOR. She is hoping that his room will be warm enough and not too warm; that it will not have the air of a room too long shut up; that the sheets will be cool and dry.

> LUCRECE *and* TARQUIN *have mounted the platform again.*
>
> *The* SERVANTS *have come forward on the right. They are whispering among themselves.*

EMILIA. Do you think she should?

SIDONIA. Is it fitting — really? — that a young man should pass the night...

EMILIA. ... when the husband's not home?

MARINA. Hasn't he any friends he can go to?

JULIA. Why should a soldier be afraid to continue his journey by night? Rome is so near...

> *The* SERVANT *reappears at the back.*

SECOND NARRATOR. Take care! Take care! Look at him now! How he gazes at her! He is possessed with admiration! His eyes devour her.

FIRST NARRATOR. Let Lord Tarquin be conducted to his room.

> *The* WOMEN *curtsey.*

19

TARQUIN. Good night, my lady.

LUCRECE. Good night, my lord.

SECOND NARRATOR. Ha! — Ha!

THE CURTAIN FALLS

> *Throughout the remainder of the play, the* NARRATORS *make use of two heavy chairs that have been placed before the proscenium pillars, one at the right and the other at the left. Each is reached by a step as though it were a pulpit.*

ACT TWO

ACT TWO

LUCRECE'S *room.*

On a platform at the back of the stage and in the centre is a great bed with a canopy. The curtains of the bed are closed.

The stage now contains eight columns arranged in a semicircle. The first and eighth columns are almost directly behind the NARRATOR'S chairs.

Calm. Tranquillity. A bell of delicate timbre strikes twelve.

The FIRST NARRATOR enters from the back at the right, carrying a large book under her arm. She walks with cautious step, but the rattling of some keys at her girdle can be faintly heard as she moves. Passing by the bed, she pauses and, bending her head, listens intently.

FIRST NARRATOR. She sleeps. She sleeps... her dark head upon the swelling pillow. One white hand rests beneath her cheek, the lily by the rose; the other hand lies along the green silk of the coverlet. This is a slumber that resembles some happy death, some tranquil and holy death. But she is breathing and her breath plays with the hair that trembles above her cheek. In a profound innocence, in a profound chastity, she lives and is asleep.

23

She mounts to her chair and sits down murmuring:

She is asleep.

She opens her great book with its red edges and, settling her elbows along the arms of her chair, she prepares for a long waking session and reads. Some time passes. The silence is unbroken save by the whisper of a turning page.

The SECOND NARRATOR enters at the left back. He crosses the stage with great caution, arrives by his chair and stands for a moment in meditation.

SECOND NARRATOR. Tarquin cannot sleep.

The FIRST NARRATOR turns a page.

This is the hour of the night when all have found sleep. Who is awake now? — thieves, and the care-ridden and those oppressed by evil desire. Tarquin is all of these! Tarquin is oppressed by evil desire. Tarquin is ridden by care. And Tarquin is... yes, he is a thief, a thief!

He takes a few steps with lowered head.

For he is contemplating... that is, he *would* be a thief, if he followed to its end the thing he purposes. But it hasn't come to that yet. (*To the audience.*) It hasn't yet reached that point, has it? — He is a king's son. He has within him the stuff from which a great ruler might be made... He is of royal stature... Is he not?

He descends to the very front of the stage and putting his hands on his hips gazes sombrely into the audience.

The FIRST NARRATOR turns a page.

The SECOND NARRATOR *starts at the noise, listens a
moment and then murmurs:*

No. It was nothing... only the footfall of the passing
night upon the pavement. But... how many such foot-
falls there must be e'er morning comes! Oh! Oh!... what
a waking night lies before us still...!

*He sits down on the lowest step that leads into the
audience, his head in his hands. Again he starts
suddenly with a shudder when the* FIRST NARRATOR
turns a page.

What is he, after all, but a man swollen with pride!
An arrogant man. Is he not the son of Tarquin the
Proud?... His envy hungers and thirsts after other
men's goods. No, it's not so much the *thing* he desires!
It's the act of *obtaining,* of having his will. It's not so
much the goal, the prize that counts. It's that every
one of his wishes must be fulfilled. And how deep a
malady of the soul is that!

*He rises, slowly paces the left lateral steps of the fore-
stage and climbs the further steps that lead to his
chair. He seats himself, heavily.*

A page is turned. He starts. Then, in anguish:

Ah! how many grains of sand there are in an hour-glass.

He heaves a profound sigh. The FIRST NARRATOR
*starts with alarm and half turns toward the bed.
Then, reassured, she murmurs:*

FIRST NARRATOR. She is asleep.

And again becomes absorbed in her book.

SECOND NARRATOR. That was an owl that cried just then. Wasn't it?... Hm — yes... it was an owl. From that direction. Hm... hm... And that's a wolf howling... over there. It's higher pitched than a dog's... shriller than a dog's. Listen: it's begun again. Ahi — ahi — ahi! Tarquin, I suppose, has engaged these musicians to enchant the nights of Lucrece. Yes, if he were given to music he would be composing for wild beasts. A sinister lover to have! A baleful suitor to have about the house! Oh, I am oppressed, I am ill at ease tonight.

FIRST NARRATOR (*putting her book down on her knees*). That bird I hear... that is a turtle-dove. Yes, that's what it is ... cooing... a turtle-dove. And how harmoniously that dog in the distance is baying at the moon! The night flows by tranquilly... sweetly...

SECOND NARRATOR (*on the forestage, to the audience*). What? ... What now?... I think that... What? Yes, he has got up... (*He listens.*) He has got out of bed. I can hear him striding back and forth in his room.

> *He starts, like* TARQUIN, *to stride to and fro.*

Consider. Pause. Come, now, let us be masters of ourself. In whom can we trust, if not in ourself? What confidence can we ever place in another, if we set about slaying our confidence in ourself? SELF! What strength should lie in that word! What assurance! What certitude!
'Tarquin? Sextus Tarquinius?'
'Here, sir!' — and promptly the struggle is at an end.

> *He walks toward the left and stops three steps from the wall.*

No. No.... It's over now. It was a test we were making. It was a game with ourself: it's over now.... Look at yourself in the glass. Use your cuirass as a mirror and consider yourself. From top to toe. And I pray you: be convinced: There are certain things that, hereafter, one cannot even think. (*As though seeing himself in a mirror.*) — A soldier! A man of iron! the slave of his flesh! Besieged, conquered, enslaved, overcome by his flesh. That's unthinkable!

Consider: dying itself would not deliver you from the results of such an act; contempt would follow you even there. The Herald would invent some degrading epithet for you. Tarquin the... Tarquin the Coward. Or the Mad. Or Tarquin the Base. Tarquin the Base, son of Tarquin the Proud? Does that suit you, then?... Remember you are a king's son, a king to be. Give a thought to the records of History!...

> *He resumes pacing back and forth, as though arguing with himself.*

Moreover, what do you gain, if you obtain the thing you contemplate? A dream... a breath... a trifle of fleeting pleasure. Who would destroy a whole vineyard to obtain one cluster? — What man would be so mad?

> *He interrupts himself abruptly, listens and adds:*

Hst! He is leaving his room.

> *He hurries to his chair, mounts to it, and, turning his face toward the back of the stage, waits anxiously.*

> *Pause.*

> TARQUIN, *half unclothed, appears at the right, directly behind the* FIRST NARRATOR, *and begins a long,*

winding progress across the stage, passing among the columns that will finally bring him out behind the SECOND NARRATOR.

The SECOND NARRATOR, *his chin resting on his folded fist, watches the first part of* TARQUIN'S *progress in silence. This progress is as follows:*

TARQUIN *appears abruptly — as though he emerged from the wall itself — between the right forward edge of the proscenium pillar and the First Column. He appears in profile, bent slightly forward, hands clenched, forehead lowered, his whole body tensely held on the watch. He slowly turns so· as to present his back to the audience and takes a cautious step forward, puts his right hand against Column One, listens, and disappears behind the column.*

The SECOND NARRATOR *releases his breath, looks into the audience with a gaze of profound concern, then resumes his position of waiting, both fists under his chin.*

SECOND NARRATOR (*striking the arms of his chair with both fists*). He sees all the doors thus trustingly left open before him! I cannot understand why this man does not return in shame to his room!

TARQUIN, *coming from the right, reappears against Column Two, falls as it were upon it. Surrounding it with his arms, he stretches his head anxiously and inquiringly around it; leaves it behind; goes rapidly to the back of the stage and makes the circuit of Column Three, left to right. Then very slowly he covers the space from Column Three to Column Four in one great step, but with the greatest caution and filled with extreme apprehension. After which he disappears behind* LUCRECE's *bed.*

TARQUIN *reappears at the left of* LUCRECE's *bed — Column Five — and slowly moves over to Column Six which hides him from the audience's view.*

But each of these doors creaks, however slightly. Every one of them. And the hinges of some of them cry out. They cry out loud. Surely that should recall him to his senses. There is nothing in the world that makes one pause like the sound of a strange door.

But TARQUIN *reappears behind Column Seven. First the audience sees his eager hands fold and intertwine themselves on the surface of the column which is offered to view; then his head, then his body emerge sideways from behind the column and glide toward the last, the Eighth, on the left, behind which he disappears.*

The very air in the halls... the very creaking of the boards beneath his feet... yes, the very odour of the house, the odour alone of this house that is unknown to him, another man's home — all that should stop him! WILL STOP HIM!

Whereupon TARQUIN *emerges directly behind the* SECOND NARRATOR. *The latter crouches back in his chair as far as possible from* TARQUIN, *who — now fully in view of the audience — pants, and with a forced laugh, wipes away the perspiration with his arm, and like an animal on the scent, takes stock of his surroundings.*

There is now only one door between Lucrece and Tarquin. Between Lucrece and this man there remains but one door.

> TARQUIN *slowly crosses the forestage until he arrives at the middle. There he stops and seems to hesitate. The* SECOND NARRATOR *sighs, as though with relief.* TARQUIN *turns toward the back and takes a large resolute step towards the platform.*

> *The* SECOND NARRATOR *rises.*

His guilty hand raises the latch. With one knee he opens the door. He enters the room! This criminal advances into the room. This criminal advances towards the bed.

> TARQUIN *mounts the platform.*

Will he dare to part the curtains?

> TARQUIN *moves about the bed.*

No, he will not dare! See, he does not dare! — It is not too late! The evil can still be repaired. It is still possible to wipe out the whole mistake!... Still...

> TARQUIN *parts the curtains. The* SECOND NARRATOR *says in a low voice:*

Oh! Savage...

FIRST NARRATOR (*fallen asleep and leaning far back in her chair*). My dear lord... away at the war... my comrade... my friend... my dear husband...

> TARQUIN *takes a step backward, covering his eyes with his hands.*

SECOND NARRATOR. He is dazzled. He is blinded. Here is trust; here is innocence. Their radiance blinds him.

> TARQUIN *remains for a moment as before.*

Would he were blind! Would that the Gods — now, suddenly — would strike him blind!...

> TARQUIN *uncovers his eyes.*

Alas, no. Such miracles no longer take place. The crime lives in his eyes, and his eyes, which might have prevented the crime, will now urge it on.

> TARQUIN *again approaches the bed. The* SECOND
> NARRATOR *continues in a low voice:*

How beautiful she is!

> TARQUIN *leans over the bed gazing at Lucrece, then
> draws himself up, steps back and contemplates her.*

FIRST NARRATOR. ... one white hand rests beneath her cheek, the lily by the rose...

SECOND NARRATOR (*softly*). ... her hand... her cheek...

FIRST NARRATOR. ... the other lies along the green silk of the coverlet... her breath plays with the hair that trembles above her cheek.

SECOND NARRATOR. ... her hair...

FIRST NARRATOR. Her breasts, blue-veined and ivory white, are like two maiden worlds...

> TARQUIN *stands in profile, one hand resting on the
> bedpost. He makes a move toward the bed.*

He broods over this poor sleeping soul and his very ecstasy moderates the fury of his lust... But now the ecstasy begins to add new fire to lust. The heart of Tarquin is a roll of drums that sounds the signal of attack. His blood rages like a torrent through his veins. His hand, smoking with desire, steals toward her breast...

> *The hand of* TARQUIN *is seen to glide toward her breast and he suddenly places it upon her.*

LUCRECE (*awaking suddenly*). Ah!

THE NARRATORS (*with raised elbow, both turn toward the wall*). Ah!

LUCRECE (*faintly*). What is it?

TARQUIN. Do you not guess?

LUCRECE. What do you wish?

TARQUIN. Do you not know?

LUCRECE. I know nothing. I can guess nothing. I am afraid. You have waked me up from a deep sleep. When I opened my eyes, I thought it was a ghost I saw. My heart has never beaten so loudly! Why are you here? What is it? What do you want?

TARQUIN. You.

LUCRECE. What is it? What do you want?

TARQUIN. You. I have come for you. It is you I want.

LUCRECE. Oh!

TARQUIN. It is you who are to blame. It is your eyes that have betrayed you to this. It is your beauty that has set a trap for you tonight. Submit, therefore, with patience to my desire. With my whole strength I have fought against this, but while reason would have prevented me, your beauty has inflamed me.

LUCRECE. Tarquin, I beseech...

TARQUIN. Be still. This is a crime; I know it. I see already the long succession of ills that will follow on what I do. I have weighed in the bottom of my soul the outrage, the shame, the woe that will result from what I do. I foresee all that will come after this night. Scorn, disdain, hatred without end. All these things I know. My thoughts since yesterday have repeated these things and repeat them still. But my desire is deaf to them.

LUCRECE. Tarquin!

TARQUIN. No! No! Listen to me, Lucrece, I know that I shall feel remorse. I know how it will come, and already I have shed the first tears of my repentance.

(*He makes a movement.*)

LUCRECE. Tarquin! Stop!

NARRATORS (*again turning toward the stage*). Stop!

33

LUCRECE. By all-powerful Jupiter! I implore you!

FIRST NARRATOR. By the grace of courtesy!

SECOND NARRATOR. By the laws of chivalry!

LUCRECE. I beseech you by my tears, Tarquin!

FIRST NARRATOR. By the laws of loyalty!

SECOND NARRATOR. By the holy claim of humanity!

LUCRECE. By the sky that is over us!

FIRST NARRATOR. By the earth!

SECOND NARRATOR. By the powers that are in it!

LUCRECE. I beg you to consider your honour and not your infamous desire!

NARRATORS. Infamous!

LUCRECE. My husband is your friend. For love of him, for love of him, spare me!

SECOND NARRATOR. You are of high station — for love of yourself, spare her.

FIRST NARRATOR. She is a child, a helpless child. Do not seize her thus by guile.
Again TARQUIN *moves.*

LUCRECE. Are you indeed Tarquin, or have you assumed his shape to destroy him? — Oh, I call on all the army of Heaven! Let it witness that it is honour that you are insulting. Consider what you are, or what you should be! A king, Tarquin, a great king!

SECOND NARRATOR. If you commit a crime like this as prince, what crimes will you commit when you are king?

FIRST NARRATOR. You will be feared, and monarchs should be loved!

SECOND NARRATOR. The crimes of kings are not buried and forgotten in the mire. Tarquin — King!

LUCRECE. Roman King!

FIRST NARRATOR
SECOND NARRATOR } King!
LUCRECE

TARQUIN. Enough!

FIRST NARRATOR
SECOND NARRATOR } King!
LUCRECE

TARQUIN. A man! A man! I am a man! This is a man who has come into your room. This is a man who enters your bed.

LUCRECE. Look! My hands implore you; they supplicate...

TARQUIN. Yes. Yes. And I take them. Give them to me
— your hands — give them to me...

LUCRECE. Wait! Listen to me...

TARQUIN. No.

> *The* NARRATORS *descend from their chairs and kneel
> with hands outstretched toward* TARQUIN.

FIRST NARRATOR
SECOND NARRATOR} Have pity!

LUCRECE. Wait but one moment! Wait! — I have a word
to say...

TARQUIN (*holding her to him*). I am listening.

> LUCRECE *pants.*

Say what you will; speak! How beautiful you are in
your tears; your sobs shake me from head to feet.
Weep! Weep! Weep into my eyes. Weep into my
mouth. Sob into my heart.

LUCRECE (*sobbing*). Ha — ha — ha —

> *The* NARRATORS *murmur in anguish.*

TARQUIN. Listen, listen to our two hearts beating against
one another. Each is as loud, each is as fast as the other.
Beat! Beat! Beat! Ah, the ecstasy of it! These hearts
within us that are ourselves and are yet unknown to us!
Wait! Wait! (*He places her body the length of his own.*)
Now yours beats the faster. No — no — no, it is mine.
Ah, the race of our two hearts as we lie thus close to-

gether! They race, I tell you, toward the same end. Never, never has your heart beat as it beats this night. Do you know what it is? Lucrece, do you know why your heart beats so?

LUCRECE. No.

TARQUIN. Listen... Let me tell you in your ear.

LUCRECE. No! No! No! (*She tears herself away from him.*) Help! Help me!

TARQUIN. Be still!

NARRATORS. Help her!

TARQUIN. Be still! (*Drawing his sword.*) Listen! If you refuse me — I shall slay you in your bed. Then I shall cut the throat of one of your meanest, lowest slaves. I shall throw his body into your dead arms, and I shall swear before the immortal gods that it was in his embrace I slew you.

LUCRECE (*falling back on the bed*). Haaaaaa. (*Exhausted.*) Haaaaaaa!

> The NARRATORS *with a gesture of imprecation veil their faces and go out.*

TARQUIN. Be still... I love you. (*He puts one knee on the bed.*) I love you. (*He leans over* LUCRECE.) I love you.

> *He takes her in his arms.*

> *Silence, save for the faint moan of* LUCRECE.

ACT THREE

ACT THREE

LUCRECE'S *room. The next morning. The curtains of the bed are drawn.*

There is a sound of joyous young voices, of whispering, and of half-suppressed bursts of laughter.

The four serving women enter from the back of the stage at the left. EMILIA *comes first; then* JULIA *with a ewer and a small silver basin;* MARINA *with some linen; and* SIDONIA *bearing a basket of fruit.*

EMILIA. Sh, I say. Not so much noise. I tell you, not so much noise. Anyone would think you were my lady's friends, and not her maids.

SIDONIA. We are! She treats us as friends. We're both.

MARINA. She told us to be like this.

JULIA. She likes to hear us laugh.

MARINA. She wants us to be happy.

EMILIA. Silence! Now that's the last time I'm going to ask for it. There's laughter and laughter. Yours is too loud. This is no ordinary house, you should remember.

They take a number of steps among the columns in silence.

41

EMILIA. Why, I don't understand it! That's the fifth door we've found wide open before us! Whose work is it to shut these doors at night?

SIDONIA ⎫
JULIA ⎭ You know very well.

MARINA. It's Valerius's!

EMILIA. Are you sure he didn't ask one of you to do it for him last night?

JULIA. No!

SIDONIA. Not me!

MARINA. No!

EMILIA. Are you certain?

SIDONIA. Not me!

JULIA. Not me!

MARINA. Certain!

EMILIA. I shall have to take it up with him.

They have reached the left portion of the forestage.

EMILIA *makes them pass before her in review.*

Julia, you must hold the basin so... level. Marina, I gave you the towels well folded so that they might keep

warm. There you go unfolding them! Hooooo-oh! So
Sidonia carries a basket of fruit under her arm now!
Why not carry it on your back like a porter?

SIDONIA *puts it on her head.*

No, not on your head either.

SIDONIA. Well, if you know so much, at the house I was in
last they always carried the fruit on their heads.

EMILIA. What an elegant house that must have been! Whose
was it?

SIDONIA. Marcius's. He writes plays. And he is very famous
and *very* hard to please.

EMILIA. Well, when next you happen to meet your former
master, you can tell him that this is the way they carry
fruit in houses that are houses. (*She holds the basket
before her in both hands; then returns it to* SIDONIA.) You
might as well know right now that my lady is as gentle
and as patient and as kind as can be. But she sees every
little mistake you make, and they displease her *greatly.*
Now let me look at you! Is everything all right?

THE WOMEN. Yes, Colonel! Yes, General!

(*They burst out laughing.*)

EMILIA (*also laughing*). Now we can go into the room. And
don't shriek 'Good morning' as though you were a
company of fish-wives.

They turn toward the bed, mount the steps of the forestage together, take a step forward and say:

ALL. Good morning, my lady!

> *They advance one more step and stop. Then turn toward the audience, and add in a low voice:*

EMILIA. Oh, she is not awake yet!

SIDONIA. But it's full daylight already.

MARINA. The streets are full of people.

JULIA. All the noises in the house have begun...

EMILIA. ... and yet she's not awake!

> *They listen. Pause.*

SIDONIA. She must have been ill.

EMILIA. She would have called me.

MARINA. Perhaps she couldn't sleep during the night...

EMILIA. Then, too, she would have called me. Every now and then she becomes anxious about her husband at the war. She calls for me and I reassure her and...

JULIA. Perhaps she has such a good and very very deep dream that she cannot find her way out of it? That happens.

EMILIA. What am I to do?

> *They all gaze at one another in doubt.*

Enter from the back at the right four menservants. The first, VALERIUS, *carries* TARQUIN'S *coat; the second, a pitcher and a cup; the third, a dressing-gown; the fourth, some bread on a great dish. They slowly come forward between the columns on the right.*

(*Softly.*) Valerius?

VALERIUS. Emilia? — What is it?

EMILIA. Not so loud! My lady is not yet awake.

VALERIUS (*lowering his voice*). What!... Not yet... why, never did...

EMILIA. It's never happened before. Every day she's ready to say Good morning to us; she's sitting up in her bed and laughing. But today the curtains are drawn

VALERIUS. That's not the first surprise today. We've just come from my Lord Tarquin's room. Nobody's there. He's gone.

THE WOMEN. Gone?...

VALERIUS. His bed hadn't even been slept in. He must have thrown himself on it fully dressed. There's mud on the counterpane. He drank the whole water pitcher; he upset the wine on the floor and he broke the glass.

EMILIA. Old soldiers act like that! You'd think he was a veteran of twenty wars!

45

VALERIUS. He must have left long ago, too. His room is cold. You'd know at once that he hadn't slept in it. And he forgot and left his coat on a chair...

> *He unfurls the coat. The men and the girls crowd about it with exclamations, feeling it and smelling it.*

THE MEN. H-h-h-h! It smells of perfume.

MARINA. Huh! — It smells of horses.

EMILIA. What a way to act! Suddenly appear at a house after ten o'clock at night when the master is away... so that the lady of the house has to ask you to stay... and then simply disappear before dawn... like a thief.

THE GIRLS (*laughing*). Valerius! Valerius! Hurry and count the silver...

VALERIUS. It's nothing to laugh about, go.

EMILIA. A messenger may have come and called him back to the camp...

VALERIUS. There is no excuse. Here! Catch that! Let it be cleaned! (*He throws* TARQUIN's *coat to a manservant.*) He could have left a letter. He could have called for me. I took care to show him the door to my room.

EMILIA. What are we to do, Valerius?

> *They turn toward the back of the stage.* EMILIA *cautiously approaches the bed, listens, and turns toward the servants. They nod to encourage her; she draws*

> *still nearer to the bed, and finally with great caution parts the curtains and looks in. Then she returns noiselessly to her companions.*

She is asleep. She must have had a nightmare; the bed is all disarranged. She lies with her head buried in her arms. As though she were ever so tired. Come, we shall let her sleep as long as she can. She must have had a nightmare.

(*To the women.*) Let her sleep as long as she likes...

(*To* VALERIUS.) Let her sleep as long as she likes....

VALERIUS. ... that's best.

> VALERIUS *nods to the men, who go out left, followed by the women.* EMILIA *stops for a moment to look back at the bed and then follows them out.*

LUCRECE. No, I am not asleep... not asleep... I shall never sleep again. Never in my life shall I find sleep again. (*She sobs.*) No, Emilia, it was not a vision, not a nightmare. It was real! All, all of it was real!

> *She falls back on the bed amid the waves of her hair.*

> *The* FIRST NARRATOR *enters on the right, behind her chair; she leans against it wearily and addresses the audience:*

FIRST NARRATOR. The monster having had his fill departed. Bent over, spent, he crawled away. And here in the shadow, in the dark, *she* remained alone, piteously alone, to weep, to sob, to hide her face in woe. How was it possible these others did not hear her, for she smote her breast in anguish, in anguish! She all but... Can't you understand? The thing that filled her most with horror was to feel her heart, still beating, still pure, within her soiled body.

LUCRECE (*raising herself*). Oh, what a wound to have received...

FIRST NARRATOR. A wound without a scar, mysterious and terrible...

LUCRECE. Myself. The very heart of myself is gone. Nothing is left of all that I treasured most in myself.

(*She sinks back on the bed.*)

FIRST NARRATOR. The roses in the bud are fed upon by worms. The springs in the forest are poisoned by the slime of frogs. The hearts of princes are visited by madness. Kings break the solemn vows they have taken. Is there no perfection to be found that does not contain within it the germ of its own decay?

She mounts to her chair and sits down.

The thought leads on and on until one despairs of everything...

She buries her head in her hands.

LUCRECE. Collatine! If it is true that your honour is deposited in my hands, know that it has been snatched from me by violence. The blame is not mine. It was for your honour that I received him into the house. It was from you he came. How could I have sent him from the door?

He complained of his fatigue... he, he talked of courage and virtue...

She sobs, sitting at the edge of the bed.

FIRST NARRATOR. Opportunity! Opportunity! It is you who are to blame for this. It is you who betray the betrayer. You it is who guide the wolf to where the lamb can be seized. Desire, however criminal it may be, cannot be fulfilled until Opportunity shows the way. All evil lies in ambush in the shadow of Opportunity waiting to seize upon the poor humble souls that pass by...

She descends to the forestage.

The patient dies while the doctor sleeps; the orphan perishes while the oppressor grows fat; justice collects its booty while the widow weeps. When will you come to the aid, not of the powerful, but of the humble, of the sick, of the poor and of the good? Envy and treachery and lust find what they seek in your sack. But Virtue...

She seats herself on the steps in the middle.

When it comes to assisting Virtue, you have no moment free. It's not convenient. It doesn't suit you. No. If it's the unforeseen you crave, Opportunity, why couldn't it have been Collatine you brought to Rome last night? In place of Tarquin...

LUCRECE *sobs.*

The FIRST NARRATOR *turns slightly toward* LUCRECE.

Unhappy child!

LUCRECE. Unhappy that I am!

The SECOND NARRATOR *appears at the left.*

SECOND NARRATOR. Tarquin!... has gone back to the camp. He rode in quite calmly, as though nothing had happened. Trumpet calls! Fanfares! Sentries salute! Guards spring to attention! Officers come out of tents!

'Good-morning!'

'It will be a splendid day! What, you lazy idlers, I've been galloping while you've been snoring. This long siege will make us rusty. Give me an attack, a charge, an assault upon some stronghold. That's the kind of war for me.'

'Hep, there, fellow! Take my horse to the stable. Curry him. Rub him down well. He's worn out.'

'Ah, Collatine! You look very well today. Yes, you look very well indeed.'

LUCRECE. Unhappy, unhappy that I am.

FIRST NARRATOR. Unhappy child!

SECOND NARRATOR. Such men have hearts of stone. Last night I saw him frowning, pitiable, with hanging cheek and glazed eye, miserable. He despised himself; he loathed himself; he cursed his transient delight. He left the house aghast at what he had done; longing for the fresh purity of dawn. Now, day has come and Tarquin has forgotten everything.

Pause. The SECOND NARRATOR *goes to the door as though he were* TARQUIN *arriving at his tent.*

I shall sleep for two hours. See that I am not disturbed. Tell those trumpeters that's enough, that will do. — You, you there, go and play your games farther off... Is there cool wine in my tent? — What? Now I remember who you are. No, I shall not remit your sentence. Fifty strokes of the rod. Fifty. That will teach you to take advantage of these country girls. Go! Away with you!... Let me be awaked at noon by my cook passing a portion of new-roasted kid before my nose.

He yawns, laughs and goes out left.

LUCRECE. Oh!... (*Sobs.*)

FIRST NARRATOR. Oh, Time, Time, that readest thy lessons to the just men as well as to the wicked, teach all just men to loathe this man.

LUCRECE. Oh! Oh!...

FIRST NARRATOR. Contrive ills beyond ill and extremities beyond extremity that will cause this man to curse the work of this crime-filled night. Trouble his hours of rest with phantoms of terror. May the host of the furies stupefy his eyes. Fill his bosom to the full with sobs, with groans.

LUCRECE. Oh!... Oh!... Oh!...

FIRST NARRATOR. May his days be passed in trembling: his nights be filled with shuddering. May all that he most fears be fulfilled.

LUCRECE (*slowly coming forward*). Oh... oh!... let him not die in battle...

FIRST NARRATOR. Give him time in which to know despair...

LUCRECE. ... To live, a slave...

FIRST NARRATOR. ... To beg from beggars those things which even a beggar rejects...

LUCRECE. I implore thee... Oh, may he feel madness coming on in terror of his own shadow. Every hour let him plan his own death, yet never achieve it.

> *She stands reaching imploringly upwards in the middle of the stage. Then her arms fall to her side; her hands twist and turn upon one another.*

This pain!... this pain!... All the words in the world cannot appease this pain! (*Louder.*) This pain! (*Crying out.*) This pain!... There are flames, there is a fire within me!... Where then... where is the means to put it out?

> *She moves about the stage, distraught; then stands suddenly motionless, her back to the audience.*

FIRST NARRATOR (*crying out*). No! No!... Not that!

LUCRECE (*returning suddenly to the front of the stage*). Unhappy arm, why do you tremble so at this decision I have taken? Take pride in this: that you are to be my deliverer. If I die, my honour lives in you. But if I live, you live and have a part in my shame. (*She stretches her arm out.*) You who were not able to defend me *then*. (*She kneels and continues in a low voice.*) Collatine, oh, my beloved Collatine, you will never know the long bitterness of doubt. I shall not insult your trusting love by asking it to offer me all the devices of an affectionate deceit... of a hypocritical indulgence. Tarquin in the secrecy of his tent shall not laugh at your uncertainty. He shall not whisper about this night among his companions in debauch. I shall recount these things with my own mouth. And while I tell them, my eyes shall weep tears that wash away the shame.

She rises.

I bequeath my honour to the blade of a knife. I bequeath my blood to Tarquin. My blood stained by him, soiled by him, shall be poured out for him. Let my testament be drawn up, and let that be his portion in it.

And you, my dear lord and husband, what shall I bequeath to you? My resolution, oh, my beloved.

My soul to heaven! My body to earth; and my good name, let it be left without fear to those that come after me.

She moves slowly to the back of the stage at the left and calls:

Emilia! Emilia!

She returns beside the bed.

A pause.

Enter EMILIA *at the left.*

EMILIA. My lady!

LUCRECE (*brokenly*). Emilia!...

EMILIA (*in consternation*). My lady!...

LUCRECE. Emilia, my good, my faithful, my unhappy Emilia...

EMILIA (*kneels weeping at her feet*). My dear mistress...

LUCRECE (*raising her up*). But, my child, why are you weeping in this way? Know, know, my dear Emilia, that if tears could cure the ill from which I suffer, my tears would long ago have been sufficient.

EMILIA. My lady, if I dared to ask... to know what it is that...

LUCRECE. No, say nothing... do not speak of it...

EMILIA. Some great misfortune has befallen this house? Is that so, my lady?

LUCRECE. A great wrong... Say nothing more... my Lord Tarquin has gone?

EMILIA. He had left before I was up, though I was up before dawn.

LUCRECE. Alas... alas...

> She weeps softly, leaning against the bed. EMILIA with lowered head weeps silently beside her. LUCRECE then dries her eyes.

And your girls... and the servants? Where are they?

EMILIA. Marina has gone to the market. Sidonia is cleaning the silver... Julia is at the linen...

LUCRECE. Yes...

EMILIA. Claudius is caring for the horses. Valerius is now working in the garden.

LUCRECE. The garden... the sun is shining. The garden must be...

EMILIA. It is beautiful, my lady. Never were there so many birds. The rain that fell last night has made it more fragrant than ever before.

LUCRECE. It rained during the night?

EMILIA. My lady did not hear it rain?

LUCRECE. No.

EMILIA. Does my lady wish us to leave the work...?

LUCRECE. No, no. The work must go on as it always has. There must be no change... ever... ever. You will make sure of that, Emilia?

EMILIA. Yes, my lady.

LUCRECE. And Emilia... this is hard to say... I wish to speak to you about... about Collatine... my husband ... Collatine, your master. He is... a great man,... so lovable, too... but he is heedless in little things. You know that; you know that?

EMILIA (*smiling*). Yes, my lady.

LUCRECE. He leaves things here and there; he disarranges things. You must quietly follow him about, putting things in place again. And when I... if I should die, do you know what my spirit would be made happy to see, as it wandered about this house? To see that you, you had inherited all my ways of doing things!

EMILIA. Oh, my lady.

LUCRECE. All, all of them, and that would not be easy. — He catches a cold so easily. You must learn the art of opening and closing windows. And his meals, Emilia! You must take such pains. He is greedy of good things, but he loses appetite so quickly. And there must be flowers and fresh flowers everywhere. And you must have a hatred of dust.

EMILIA. I have, my lady.

LUCRECE. But not enough, but not enough. It is so stealthy an enemy. Drive it from the door, it will return by the window. You leave a spotless room; you return in five minutes: it is all to be done again. No, no, one must not carry the thing to an absurdity, as some do. But a house that is beautifully ordered, oh, my dear Emilia, that is a task that never ends. You will remember these things — now you shall help me dress.

> EMILIA *starts to leave the room.*

But there is another thing I was forgetting. You must watch very carefully over your master's clothes! You know him there, too. He would put on a white tunic in the middle of December, and his cloak that is lined with fur at the end of July. He would gallop off to camp in the shoes he had worn at a banquet. I know you will take great care of that. Now find me a dress.

EMILIA. Which dress would my lady wear?

LUCRECE. Emilia, see... that black dress... the dress my mother wore in mourning. Today, as you see, I am more unhappy than you can know. That dress will suit me beyond any other.

EMILIA (*amazed and overcome*). My lady... my lady... I feel I have the right to implore you...

LUCRECE. No, be still, my child. Let me bear my grief alone. It is easy to be a great lady in good fortune — to be a great lady by birth and by high place; but today I must be a great lady in misfortune. Go now! and send Valerius to me.

> EMILIA *goes out at the right.*

Oh, Rome! Roman legend, history! Latin tongue and Latin dignity! Roman soul! What preparation and what example you have given us for misfortune! I have not slept. I have suffered; I have shed all the tears that my body held; and yet now I feel myself strong and able. My heart beats with an even beat. All the happy hours of my life — I now see — flowed like a great river to make up this sea of troubles on which I am shipwreck. Am I to cast about for hope and help? No, I shall sink from sight calmly and serenely.

One morning, as I was sailing on the bay of Baiae, I saw a statue of Minerva at the bottom of the sea, the last remainder of some ship that foundered a hundred years before. I must now hold before my eyes, until the end, the memory of that white marble statue, seated, like the mother of silence, among the weeds that grow at the bottom of the sea.

Knocking at the door.

Yes?

Enter VALERIUS *from the left.*

My good Valerius, you are to saddle the white horse.

VALERIUS. My lady, that is impossible. Last night the white horse was savagely bitten by Lord Tarquin's horse.

LUCRECE (*with hatred*). Ha-haaaaa...!

VALERIUS. I can saddle the bay...

LUCRECE. She is old...

VALERIUS. She can still do good service, my lady.

LUCRECE. You will speed to Ardea.

VALERIUS. That is some distance.

LUCRECE. You will speed to Ardea. And as quickly as possible, Valerius.

VALERIUS. Yes, my lady.

LUCRECE. You will present yourself before your master. And you will say to him: 'Greetings to my Lord Collatine, noble husband, from his unworthy wife...'

VALERIUS. My lady!

LUCRECE. '... from his unworthy wife who speaks to you now in my person. If you desire to see once more your Lucrece, deign to return to her with all possible speed. With all her strength she calls to you from the halls of your unhappy house.' Go quickly, my good Valerius, quickly.

> VALERIUS *prepares to leave, but stands aside to admit the four serving women, then leaves at the right.*

> EMILIA *draws forward a stool upon the platform at the foot of the bed.* SIDONIA, MARINA, *and* JULIA *curtsey.*

THREE SERVANTS (*in a low voice*). Good morning, my lady.

LUCRECE (*in a clear, untroubled voice*). Good morning, my friends.

> *She sits down on the stool.* EMILIA *tends to her hair,* MARINA *to her hands, and* JULIA *puts on her shoes.* SIDONIA *stands waiting, motionless, the black dress across her arms.*

LUCRECE. What? You have nothing to say this morning?

THE WOMEN (*in a low voice*). No, my lady.

LUCRECE. But yes. But where are those little things you are accustomed to tell me, those delightful, unimportant things that fill this room every morning with a sound like the twittering of birds? What, nothing of that today?

THE WOMEN (*in a low voice*). No, my lady.

LUCRECE. Come, come...

THE WOMEN. No... no, my lady.

LUCRECE. Good. So be it. But I, I have a piece of news for you... news that will be a surprise to you. Before the new year, Emilia is to marry Valerius.

EMILIA. Oh!

THE WOMEN. Emilia!

MARINA. We suspected it, my lady.

JULIA. Yes, we did, my lady.

SIDONIA. We suspected it all the time.

LUCRECE. Everyone felt it *might* be, but no one knew it.

THE WOMEN (*in a low voice, but delightedly*). Oh, she's been keeping it secret all the time!... Emilia!

LUCRECE. She, herself, didn't know it.

She rises. SIDONIA *takes a step forward.* EMILIA *hands her the dress.*

We must prepare a beautiful wedding.... Very joyous ... very young... very gay.

CURTAIN

ACT FOUR

ACT FOUR
SCENE ONE

*Before the curtain. At the opening of the act
the murmur of a crowd is heard in the distance.*

The SECOND NARRATOR *enters from the left
upon the forestage.*

SECOND NARRATOR. Some great event is in the air and
Romans are awaiting it expectantly. This morning on
leaving their houses they noticed, every one of them,
that they had crossed the threshold left foot first and
their hearts stood still with premonition. They went
back and came out again, right foot first: thus losing
one step till the evening when they will pick it up
again. They will walk warily today, for they all feel
that some great event is in the air. Their eyes are ques-
tioning, they cup their hands behind their ears, and
whatever their errand is, it seems to require their passing through the Forum.

FIRST NARRATOR (*entering from right*). The servants have
been engaged in making a bonfire at the bottom of the
garden. They have been burning the sheets and pillows,
the mattress and the green silk counterpane of a bed.

SECOND NARRATOR. Valerius, who left the courtyard at a
trot on the old mare, has returned from the camp at a
gallop on a cavalry charger. On the road from Ardea

come Collatine and Brutus, at full speed. Brutus tries to divert Collatine with his jests, but he does not succeed.

First Narrator. Lucrece...

Second Narrator (*interrupting her*). Tarquin!... (*To the* First Narrator.) I beg your pardon...

First Narrator. No, no... Tarquin?

Second Narrator. Tarquin lies sleeping in his tent... snoring amid his black curls.

First Narrator. Lucrece is in her room. She is robed in black. There she stands in black. She cannot rest. Never again will she rest in this world.

Second Narrator. Great things are in the air...

First Narrator (*interrupting him*). ... woeful things, unhappy things...

Second Narrator. Great things!

First Narrator. Unhappy things!

Second Narrator. Unhappy and great things!

First Narrator. Great and unhappy things!

> *Pause.*

Cries of a Crowd (*in the wings*). Haaaaaa!

SECOND NARRATOR. Listen!

A VOICE (*in the wings, as of a herald, indistinct, but filling the measure of a line of blank verse*).

. . . .

SECOND NARRATOR. It has begun!

ANOTHER VOICE (*farther off, interrogatively*). . . . .? (*Four syllables.*)

ANOTHER (*still farther, affirmatively*). . . . . . . (*Three syllables.*)

SECOND NARRATOR. Do you hear that?

FIRST NARRATOR. Alas!

SECOND NARRATOR. Rumour is flying through the streets of Rome. It is hard to say what the rumour is, but it can be heard, it can be seen in its flight. It passes over the city like the wind passing over a field of high grass.

CROWD
}
(*in the wings*). What's happened?
(*farther off*). What's happened?
(*successively remoter*). What's happening?

There is a roll of drums in the distance.

The SECOND NARRATOR *has followed with lifted ear the withdrawal of the voices. At the sound of the drums he mounts to his chair.*

SECOND NARRATOR. Look, Rome is in labour with History. Athens in its time was beauty. Babylon was luxury, and

67

Troy was doom. There will come a day when Paris will
be Revolution and when Berlin will be war. But Rome,
today, is History...

THE CROWD. Aye! Aye!

SECOND NARRATOR. What high destiny to be a Roman now,
when every step he takes is History! (*With enthusiasm.*)
Haaaaa!

THE CROWD. Haaaaaaa!

    Slight pause.

FIRST NARRATOR. A woman is about to die... a gracious and
gentle woman.

SECOND NARRATOR. A great and noble woman.

FIRST NARRATOR. A woman is about to take her own life.

SECOND NARRATOR. Ah, that is heroic.

FIRST NARRATOR. It is unjust. She is about to take her own
life.

SECOND NARRATOR. Yes.

FIRST NARRATOR. It is a fearful thing.

SECOND NARRATOR. Yes... It is a fearful thing.

FIRST NARRATOR. Is that all you can find to say?

SECOND NARRATOR. What is there to say? It's all written down. It's all written down in that great book of yours.

He points to the book the FIRST NARRATOR *has left in her chair at the close of the Second Act.*

FIRST NARRATOR. No, no, it's not there I read it.

SECOND NARRATOR. But read it, read it. Page fifty-two;... Cultrum quem sub veste abditum habebat...'

FIRST NARRATOR. I do not understand it.

SECOND NARRATOR. '... eum in corde defigit...'

FIRST NARRATOR. I do not understand a word of it.

SECOND NARRATOR. That's Livy. Titus Livy, his History of Rome.

FIRST NARRATOR. No, no, no. That's not the way the thing took place. Not with all that pomp and that coldness — Listen! (*Gently.*) Listen! (*Tenderly.*) 'Poor bird...'

SECOND NARRATOR. What? What is that?

FIRST NARRATOR. That is Shakespeare. 'Poor frighted deer...'

SECOND NARRATOR. But I don't understand it.

FIRST NARRATOR:
'As the poor frighted deer, that stands at gaze
Wildly determining which way to fly;

69

Or one encompass'd with a winding maze,
That cannot tread the way out readily;
So with herself is she in mutiny,
To live or die...'
She was lost in indecision. Can you see that? She hes-
itated... She... she hesitates.

SECOND NARRATOR. But it's a matter of courage, my poor
friend...

FIRST NARRATOR (*interrupting him*). It's courageous, is it, to
go and thrust yourself into a hole beneath some great
funerary monument?

She descends from her chair. He follows her.

SECOND NARRATOR. But History... History...

FIRST NARRATOR. You tire me out with your History. What
can Death do? What kind of remedy is that? Yes, yes,
there's a fine transaction for you... to buy your way out
of all the ills of life with the price of a death!

SECOND NARRATOR. Come now, consider...

FIRST NARRATOR. You are going to tell me there is no choice;
she must die... Oh, let us permit her to live! Yes, she
can go somewhere... she and Collatine, they can go into
the country.

SECOND NARRATOR. With that scar, that wound in her side?

FIRST NARRATOR. Yes, under the trees, in the long grass, the songs of the birds all about her. She will be well hidden. Collatine has a generous heart.

SECOND NARRATOR. A generous heart! He will need it!

FIRST NARRATOR. Ah, poor bird... poor frighted deer... Sad sister of Philomel... Philomel, the nightingale, whose song tells forever of her dark violation. Philomel and Lucrece, sisters in that one wrong.

> *The* SECOND NARRATOR *interrupts her with a note of impatience.*

What advantage could her death afford? Of what use, what good, would it be? I put the question to you. (*She turns to the audience and raises her mask.*) Answer me! What criminal would hesitate upon the threshold of his crime because of her death? Would one man be restrained by the step she contemplates? What? None? Then let Lucrece seek out some profound solitude, far from the highroads, and there each night the bird, her sister, will teach her once more to sing.... You are willing.

> *Sounds of an approaching crowd in the wings.*

SECOND NARRATOR. Hssh!... Listen!

FIRST NARRATOR (*to the audience*). You are willing? You are willing?

SECOND NARRATOR. Come, gather your courage together...

> *Louder sounds in the wings.*

FIRST NARRATOR (*lowering her mask*). Alas!

THE CRIES (*drawing nearer*). Haaa!... Haaa!... Haaa!...

SECOND NARRATOR. Listen!

> *They mount into their chairs and fix their gaze upon the entrance to the stage at the left, whence come the noises.*

WOMEN'S VOICES. Lucrece's house. Hurry. — Behind these stone walls of the nobles, we know what takes place... Shameful things... Shameful... Beat on the doors... Let us break in...

MEN'S VOICES. Slowly there... in order... in line... Silence ... it may not be true; we don't know yet for certain ... silence...

> *Enter* VALERIUS, *parting the curtains at the centre of the stage.*

VALERIUS (*to the crowd*). Be still, be silent, there! — Move away from the porch... Move back from there!

A WOMAN'S VOICE. There's no law against standing in the street.

VALERIUS. The houses belong to their owners at least... Your brayings have shaken the house from top to bottom.

THE WOMAN. Good! That's what we tried to do. Again, my sisters, shout!

THE WOMEN. Yes. Hahahaha!

A Man. Silence, you women. Put a rein on yourselves, you
mares.

Valerius. Well said, sir.

The Women. Hahaha!

First Narrator. Shameless... shameless curiosity.

Murmurs in the crowd.

Second Narrator. No, it is not mere curiosity that has
brought them here. Still less is it seeking after scandal
... No, it is the high Roman thirst for decorum, —
for justice and order and decorum. It is a true Roman
quality and from time to time in the arid stretches of her
history, it arises in them, as now.

The Man. Speak, Valerius.

Voices in the Crowd. Yes, speak. What has happened?
What has happened here?

Valerius. I know nothing. And if there are things I am
beginning to surmise, do you expect me to pour them
into your ears, now and here? Go back to your homes.
Before the houses of the sick and the dying, even the
happiest passer-by lowers his voice. Go then in silence.
In this house there is someone sick and at the point of
death.

The Women. Lucrece? Is it Lucrece?

Valerius. Sh!...

He goes out.

THE CROWD (*as it withdraws*). To the Forum!... To the Forum!

SECOND NARRATOR. To the Forum! Throw aside your work, all you carpenters and painters, shoemakers and tailors. Everyone to the Forum. Slaves as well, let the slaves follow too; and the women, the women as well. For it is liberation that is in the air.

FIRST NARRATOR. Let the women return to their homes. I know the old song the men will be singing in the market-place: 'Down with tyranny — death to tyrants.' But if the table is not laid at noon, the women will have their own tyrants to answer to... let them return to their homes.

SECOND NARRATOR. To the Forum!

FIRST NARRATOR. To their homes!

SECOND NARRATOR. Fill the Forum! Full! Full! Let it be one great sea of human beings!... Listen! —

A voice can be heard in the distance.

He is saying that the crimes that princes commit are doubly criminal!

Cheers in the distance.

THE CURTAIN RISES

SCENE TWO

The TWO NARRATORS *seat themselves as the curtain rises. The stage is arranged as for the Second Scene of the First Act: a room in* COLLATINE'S *house.*

SIDONIA *and* JULIA *are talking together in low tones, forward at the right.*

VALERIUS *at the back, left, has just given a command to a manservant, who stands before him.*

VALERIUS. Do you understand?

THE SERVANT. Yes.

VALERIUS. Good. Then, go.

The SERVANT *bows and goes out.*

MARINA *enters, forward left, carrying a cup on a tray. She starts to cross the stage, diagonally, but is stopped by* VALERIUS.

Marina, come here... Is that for my lady?

MARINA. Yes, Valerius.

VALERIUS. What is it?

MARINA. Milk.

VALERIUS (*two fingers on the cup*). Was it to be lukewarm?

MARINA. No, no. Hot.

VALERIUS. Feel it... It's almost cold. Go and see that it's hot.

MARINA. But my lady refuses to drink it, anyway. It was Emilia who asked for it. My lady won't touch a thing.

VALERIUS. Nevertheless, it must be hot.

> MARINA *goes out at the left.*

Julia!... Sidonia!... What are you doing there in the corner?

SIDONIA (*in distress*). Nothing, nothing! Valerius. We don't know where to go, nor what to do.

VALERIUS. What, tears?

SIDONIA. Yes... we love her. Very much.

VALERIUS. It's not for you to weep. Your task is to surround my lady with tranquillity and with silence. That is the way for a servant to show her love. Go.

> *They start to go.*

The sound of your broom on the pavement, a glimpse of household linen being put in place, or of a freshly shining plate can do more to draw your mistress from her present state than all the tragic weeping in the world.

They go out.

Enter another MANSERVANT.

THE SERVANT. Valerius!

VALERIUS. I'm not deaf!

THE SERVANT (*lower*). Valerius!

VALERIUS. Well, what is it?

THE SERVANT. The cook sent me; he wants the keys to the wine-cellar.

VALERIUS. Well, there at least is someone who is going about his work as usual. Tell him there will be no wine at dinner.

THE SERVANT. But...

VALERIUS. And there's no need to talk things over with the scullery boys. Say what you have to say, then turn on your heels and return to your work.

> MARINA *returns. She carries her cup of hot milk to* VALERIUS.

Good. By the time you reach her room it will be right.

> MARINA *starts to leave.*

What? You should dry your eyes first.

MARINA. I keep drying them all the time.

VALERIUS. Then dry them once for all.

MARINA. Yes, Valerius.

VALERIUS (*following her*). If my lady drinks the milk, I shall see to it that you receive a reward.

MARINA. Thank you, Valerius. If she drank the milk, I think the sight of it would be reward enough.

> *She goes out.*

> *Re-enter* SIDONIA *and* JULIA.
> *They cross the stage at the back without seeing* VA-
> LERIUS. *They are whispering happily together.*
> JULIA *is carrying a pail of water and* SIDONIA *has
> a broom over her shoulder.*

SIDONIA. Look out, you're spilling it all. Soon there won't be any water left in the pail.

> *They go out.*

VALERIUS (*coming forward*). They are consoled already... They are young. One cannot expect them to...

> *Enter* EMILIA *from the right.*

EMILIA. She is drinking the milk.

VALERIUS. Good.

EMILIA (*breaks into sobbing*). Oh, forgive me, Valerius... I've been smiling and smiling... for two hours up there ... two hours without failing once...

VALERIUS. My poor Emilia....

EMILIA. Let me weep now. It's like taking off a mask. But *she*... she is as brave as she is good.

VALERIUS. Yes.

SECOND NARRATOR (*rising abruptly*).   Collatine is here! Collatine on horseback!

FIRST NARRATOR (*in a low voice*). Collatine...

SECOND NARRATOR. Make room! Make way for Collatine!

FIRST NARRATOR. He is pale.

SECOND NARRATOR. May the Gods grant that he have no cause to blush.

BOTH NARRATORS. Collatine! — Collatine! — Long live Collatine!

FIRST NARRATOR. Who is the officer riding beside him?

SECOND NARRATOR. Hahaha! That is Brutus!

THE CROWD (*in the wings*). Hahahaha! Brutus! Brutus!

VOICES IN THE CROWD. Have Brutus tell us a story... Brutus, have you any jokes? — Do that trick for us on the horse, Brutus. Tell us... tell us about the beautiful Lucrece.

THE CROWD. Haha! Lucrece!

> *Laughter in the wings.*

EMILIA. I must go up to her again.

VALERIUS. Yes... We shall persuade her in time... you will see...

SIDONIA (*entering forward at the right*). My lord has come.

VALERIUS (*to Emilia*). Go up quickly.

> *Exit* EMILIA, *running.*

JULIA (*entering at the left, middle*). My lord has come.

VALERIUS. Yes... quietly, quietly...

A MANSERVANT (*entering forward left*). My lord has come.

VALERIUS. Yes, yes.

> *Enter from the left, middle,* COLLATINE *and* BRUTUS.

COLLATINE. Where is my lady?

VALERIUS. In her room, my lord.

COLLATINE. Is she ill?

VALERIUS. No, my lord.

BRUTUS. Not ill, you are sure?

VALERIUS. No, no, my lord.

BRUTUS. There, you see — all is well.

COLLATINE. Let us go up.

VALERIUS. If I may beg your pardon, my lord, but my lady has requested that my lord wait for her here.

COLLATINE. What is the matter; what has happened, Valerius?

VALERIUS. My lord, I do not know.

BRUTUS. Why, nothing at all.

COLLATINE. It is you who came to the camp with the message for me?

VALERIUS. Yes, my lord.

COLLATINE. I was away at drill. My lieutenant brought me your message. I think he must have exaggerated. Did you say you came from our *unhappy* house?

VALERIUS. I... I do not remember now.

COLLATINE. What, you... you who are Memory personified ... Exactitude itself. (*To* BRUTUS.) There are times when one could wish to have servants with less discretion.

VALERIUS. I think I may have said: 'sad'...'from your sad house.'

BRUTUS. There, you see: Lucrece is weary; she is bored.

LUCRECE

COLLATINE. It is not like her... Do you think she is one of these women who ... (*He interrupts himself and takes a step toward the women.*) But these girls have been weeping!...

THE SERVING WOMEN. No, my lord.

COLLATINE. They are ready to begin weeping again at any moment. I can see it in their eyes... But come, let us go up.

> *He takes a step forward, but* LUCRECE *enters. She is dressed in black and is supported by* EMILIA *and* MARINA. *They help her to ascend the platform, then return and stand at the right.*

> COLLATINE *slowly approaches* LUCRECE, *mounting the platform at the centre of the stage. At a sign from* VALERIUS *all the* SERVANTS *withdraw except* EMILIA. BRUTUS *stands on the lower level at the left.*

> COLLATINE *takes* LUCRECE'S *hands and gazes at her.* VALERIUS *and* EMILIA *lower their heads.* COLLATINE *draws* LUCRECE *to him and kisses her passionately.* VALERIUS *and* EMILIA *prepare to leave the stage.*

LUCRECE (*releasing herself from* COLLATINE'S *embrace*). No, no. Stay — Permit, my lord, that they stay.

COLLATINE. Yes.

> LUCRECE *moves slightly away from* COLLATINE *and gazes at him.*

COLLATINE. What strange unhappiness is it, my Lucrece,

that has left you trembling so? And what grief has been able to drive all those beautiful colours from my beloved? Why this mourning? My treasure, my beloved, tell us what it is, so that we can find its remedy at once.

LUCRECE. I... I thought I was ready... Now you must let me pause a little longer...

COLLATINE (*tenderly*). Yes, yes...

> LUCRECE *sobs.*

> *Sounds of the crowd in the wings.*

> COLLATINE *continues to* VALERIUS:

Go drive these people in the street away.

LUCRECE. No, no, no! It is the voice of the crowd that gives me courage. It is those Roman voices that have led me to say what I have to say. Let the house be open wide to those pitiless judges.

COLLATINE. My dear wife...

LUCRECE. So it must be, my dear lord. Open wide the doors, Valerius.

> *Exit* VALERIUS, *left. The noise of the crowd increases.*

Let them come in.

> *The noise increases.*

COLLATINE. But let them come in silence.

> *Sudden silence.*

LUCRECE. Let them fill the halls. Let them stand there and be my judge, without hatred and without pity, let them judge me from this day forever.

> VALERIUS *returns on tiptoe.*

A few words will be enough... my wrongs are more numerous than my words... if I were to tell you all that I have suffered, my voice would not be equal to the task... My dear lord, a stranger... a stranger...

COLLATINE (*gently*). ... a stranger?...

LUCRECE. ... came... last night...

COLLATINE. ... last night?

LUCRECE. No. I cannot...

> *She sobs.* EMILIA *supports her.*

THE CROWD (*in the wings*). A stranger, in this house, last night.

BRUTUS (*low*). Silence.

COLLATINE (*to* VALERIUS). Someone came to the house last night?

VALERIUS. Yes, my lord, the Lord Tarquin.

COLLATINE. Tarquin was here? (*To* BRUTUS.) Tarquin? That was strange. (*To* VALERIUS.) Not last night, but the night before — with the rest of us.

VALERIUS. No, no, my lord. Last night. He came again.

THE CROWD. Tarquin came here last night.

COLLATINE. Strange!

BRUTUS. Ah, I see it now! I think I see. Ah! Ah! He feels
ripe for royalty — he told me so himself. He said the
thought kept him awake at night. Yes, that's it. He
thinks the climate of Rome is injurious to his royal
father.

> *The crowd laughs.*

He holds that the chill of exile would improve the old
man.

> *Laughter.*

But as he is aware that the rest of us are simple-minded
enough to remain loyal, he proposed to go about his plans
in the long way. He hopes to reach us through our wives.

> *Laughter.*

COLLATINE. Come, enough.... (*To* VALERIUS.) At what
time did he come?

VALERIUS. At ten o'clock, my lord.

COLLATINE. Good. — Did he speak with my lady?

VALERIUS. Yes, my lord.

COLLATINE. Alone with her?

VALERIUS. No, here before us all.

COLLATINE. What did he say?

VALERIUS (*hesitating*). ... Emilia?

EMILIA (*in tears*). That urgent matters called him to Rome.

BRUTUS. Hoh!

EMILIA. That the cares that go with royalty...

BRUTUS. Tssst! Not so fast, royal cub!

> *Laughter.*

> (*To* COLLATINE.) Do you see? It's perfectly clear.

LUCRECE. Alas! Alas!

COLLATINE. Good. (*To* VALERIUS.) Whereupon Tarquin left the house?

BRUTUS. Yes, and poor lady here...

VALERIUS. No, my lord.

> *Sobs of* LUCRECE *and* EMILIA, *who cling to one another.*

COLLATINE ⎫
BRUTUS ⎭ What?

VALERIUS. My Lord Tarquin remained here.

COLLATINE⎱ What?
BRUTUS ⎰

VALERIUS. He stayed.

COLLATINE (*sharply*). Here?

VALERIUS. Yes.

COLLATINE. The night? (Yes.) All night? (Yes.) Slept here? (Yes.) Slept here, the whole night?

A WOMAN'S VOICE (*in the wings*). Ha! Ha! Ha!

BRUTUS (*to the crowd, half drawing his sword*). By Jupiter! If anyone here...

COLLATINE. When I saw him this morning, on horseback ... This morning when I saw him return to the camp, it was from here he came? Oh, oh, Lucrece, could he have dared to speak to you... to have talked to you... of love!... Hooooooo!

LUCRECE *sobs*.

But then, that's nothing. My beloved, my treasure, there... I swear to you... the shame of it falls back on him alone. He is unable to see a woman, without beginning at once to imagine... there, there! Everyone knows that... Lucrece, my beloved, do not weep so. Come, now, come, come, there is no cause to weep without ceasing... Why?... Why?... (*Suddenly.*) Haaaaah! — What! — It is not possible! What! What! Brutus!

BRUTUS. My friend!

COLLATINE. Haaaaaah!

LUCRECE. He held his sword against my heart. He said:
'If you resist me, I shall kill you. I shall cut the throat
of one of your lowest, meanest slaves. I shall throw his
body into your dead arms, and I shall swear before the
immortal Gods that it was in his embrace I slew you.'

THE CROWD. Haaaaah!

LUCRECE. I implored... I wept... I sobbed...

EMILIA. My lady!...

COLLATINE (*in a colourless voice*). He would not listen, is
that it? He did not wish to hear! He followed the
monster within him... to the fulfilment of his plan.

> LUCRECE *turns and veils her face.*

Ah, wretched! (*Changing his tone.*) Tell me — tell me:
to the fulfilment of his desire. Is that it? Is that it?
To the fulfilment...?

BRUTUS. See her... look!

> *He leaps forward, but too late.* LUCRECE *sinks to the
> ground.* EMILIA *and* COLLATINE *kneel beside her.*

THE CROWD. Haaaaah!

VALERIUS. Sh...!

EMILIA. She is dead.

VALERIUS (*to the Crowd*). She is dead!

> *Silence.*

> BRUTUS *mounts the platform, bends over* LUCRECE, *then comes to the middle of the platform. He turns half to the crowd and half to the audience.*

BRUTUS. She is dead. Tarquin has slain her. Before your eyes Tarquin has slain her. Yes, he is sleeping, over there, at Ardea in his tent; but it is here that he lives and acts. He is here before your eyes in this deed.

Do you see him entering this house, as he entered it last night... the monster, the wild boar...?

THE CROWD. Haaaah!

BRUTUS. When has he dared to bring against an enemy's city the guile, the violence, the passion that he brought here, against this woman? And this woman was the wife of his friend. Is that a man or a beast?

THE CROWD. A monster!

BRUTUS. I kiss the blade of this knife. By my lips let it receive the kiss of you all. My lips alone will be red, but you will all feel between your own the taste of blood.

> *He kisses the knife.*

Behold! Behold! I shall not wipe this blood from my lips, until the lips of Tarquin are pale in death.

THE CROWD. Death to Tarquin. Death to him!

BRUTUS (*to* COLLATINE). Rise, my friend. We have work to do.

> *He stoops and takes up the body of* LUCRECE *in his arms.*

There is another woman, like this woman, pure and noble, whom Tarquin insults daily. Daily he violates the mother of us all: Rome, Rome!

> *There is a roll of drum, and a sound of bells.*

THE CROWD. Rome! Rome! Rome!

FIRST NARRATOR (*descending from her chair and crossing the stage*). 'Poor bird... poor bird...'

SECOND NARRATOR (*doing the same*). 'Poor stricken deer...'

CURTAIN